40 Days and 40 Nights

Other Books by Ilene Segalove and Paul Bob Velick

List Your Self

More List Your Self

List Your Self for Parents
(with Gareth Esersky)

List Your Creative Self

Risk Your Self

Other Books by Ilene Segalove

Unwritten Letters

List Your Self for Pregnancy
(with Gareth Esersky)

List Your Self for Kids
(with Charlotte Blumenfeld)

The Write Mood

40 Days and 40 Nights

TAKING TIME OUT FOR
SELF-DISCOVERY

Ilene Segalove

**Andrews McMeel
Publishing, LLC**
Kansas City

08 RR4 10 9

ISBN-13: 978-0-7407-4203-3
ISBN-10: 0-7407-4203-5
www.andrewsmcmeel.com

Book design by Desiree Mueller

ATTENTION: SCHOOLS AND BUSINESSES

Andrews McMeel books are available at quantity discounts with bulk purchase for educational, business, or sales promotional use. For information, please write to: Special Sales Department, Andrews McMeel Publishing, LLC, 4520 Main Street, Kansas City, Missouri 64111.

Disclaimer

The movements and activities described in this book are solely for educational use. The author and publisher do not intend to present any part of this work as a diagnosis or prescription, nor are they responsible for anyone misrepresenting the material by such claim. Consult your medical professional before beginning any movement program. The creators of this product do not assume liability for injury or loss in connection with this exercise program and instructions therein.

I would like to dedicate this book to Rabbi Ted Falcon,
who helped me appreciate the subtle beauty
and mystery of trusting my inner experience,
and to Stephan Merritt and Sheila Dunn-Merritt,
who made sure I wasn't alone along the way.

CONTENTS

PREFACE: MY STORY

In 1996 I was trying to end a messy relationship. In the spring, I flew from Los Angeles to Seattle to spend a full day with a rabbi who was also a therapist. I was desperate to gather the strength and clarity to get unstuck and find myself. We spent two hours together as I told my story. The rabbi remained silent for most of the session. Then, in the last few minutes, he opened his eyes and spoke to me.

"You need to take 40 days and 40 nights and go into the desert of your heart and soul. Just like Moses—wait, and listen. Extricate from the drama of the 'he said, she said,' and step into something larger."

I was stunned. "You mean I should make a reservation for the overpriced Death Valley Inn?" I didn't get it.

The rabbi laughed. "I'm talking about going inside and wandering in your own psychic wilderness. Take a very specific piece of time and use it to build a container for yourself. You don't need to fast or keep a vow of silence. You simply need to commit to the truth."

On some intuitive level this suggestion made sense. I actually felt an instant craving to put myself somewhere remote and desolate to rediscover me again. I had lost the very essence of myself inside of a tumultuous love affair that had gone on way too long. Could I find my way back home?

I asked the rabbi to tell me how this desert thing worked. "The desert has been the preferred place for self-inquiry throughout the ages. Stripped bare of your daily distractions, you'll risk stepping outside of your comfort zone. You don't speak with him. You disengage from habit. The most important piece is choosing to not know what may or may not happen. That's your intention, learning to live in uncertainty. It's about trusting, tuning into your intuition, and really listening."

I counted out 40 days on my calendar and called a friend who lived in Hawaii. "Can I visit awhile?" I asked, realizing the desert was a metaphor for time out no matter where. I had work that I could easily bring along and so when she said yes, I flew over.

Day one was spent in the air. Groundless. How perfect. Day two I swam, cried, and worried. In the past I might have labeled this kind of behavior escapism. Was I running away from my problems? Not this time. This was a conscious choice, and I kept my intention to live in uncertainty alive as I kept track of what was going on in a small journal.

For the first 10 days I stopped trying to solve my so-called problems by obsessively reviewing them over and over in my mind. I floated in warm water, worked on a couple of writing projects, and rested a lot. Day 10 seemed like the beginning and end of a mini-excursion. But Day 11 felt different, somehow. That was the day I flew home, vowing to keep my commitment for 40 days.

I was tempted to reengage with the boyfriend. There was a voice in my head egging me on. "Come on, just call him. What harm can it do?" But another stronger part of me knew I was already 10 days in. I didn't want to go back on my commitment and so I held the course. I stopped answering the phone and began reading more. I tended the garden and baked pies. I slowed down considerably and went to bed pretty close to sunset. I watched lots of TV and fell in love with all kinds of sitcom and police story characters. I didn't pray. I didn't meditate. I didn't engage in any elaborate rituals or inner work. I paid my bills, handed in my work assignments, and made my bed almost every day. I didn't fall apart, well, maybe a little, and I did change.

Around Day 14 I remembered the rabbi's version of the story of Moses wandering in the desert, and his encounter with the burning bush. A bush was on fire in the desert—what was the big deal? But because Moses had nowhere else to go, because he wasn't rushing around or hanging out with his friends, he had the time and the space to pay attention. He took notice and realized this burning bush did not burn up! What was that all about? When Moses actually stopped and really listened, he realized he was in the presence of God. And God had a message for him. The rabbi informed me this major moment meant Moses had become profoundly aware of something beyond his own personal trials and tribulations. By taking the time to pay attention to what *appeared* to be ordinary, he discovered the extraordinary.

On Day 26 I was enjoying myself but also turning into a bit of a hermit, so I called the rabbi to check in. He assured me that in a week or so I might reopen the doors and have friends over for dinner to chat endlessly and share stories and laughs. But he reminded me it was still Day 26 and it was important for me to observe this piece of time inside of the sacred container that I had built for myself. I must admit, I was becoming more sensitive to the nuances of daily life. I realized how my behavior used to be driven from the outside in and how much more satisfying it felt to be fed from the inside out. This new space opened me up to some fear and trembling but also made room for great delight and surprise.

On Day 36 I remember stepping outside in the early morning and seeing the star Venus shine so brightly it was almost blinding. What was happening? I had made a decision to pay attention, to notice life instead of getting caught up in habit and routine. And it occurred to me I was no longer invested in the so-called right solution or just making it to the end of 40 days. Something else was going on.

On Day 40 I woke up and was drawn to the telephone as if it were a powerful magnet. For a split second an odd feeling washed over me. I wanted to call the boyfriend (or old boyfriend) and instantly reengage. This knee-jerk reaction took me by surprise, but just as quickly I snapped out of it and dashed outside for a brisk walk. I returned focused and filled with my newfound strength. I re-read my journal, made some notes of the me before and the me after the 40-day excursion, and was amazed! By consciously creating space and holding my intention, I had actually expanded my options, had transformed my life, and felt great!

Forty days and 40 nights was manageable, magical, and usually enjoyable. Like a symphony or play or novel, it had a very definite beginning, middle, and end. The definable shape helped me feel safe enough to let go and take a chance on change. I could experience what was happening without worrying, because I knew it would be over. As Day 40 approached I felt a huge sense of success. I had done it! I kept my intention and had finally satisfied my secret yearning to grow beyond my habits and comfort zone into something bigger and more meaningful.

I called "him" on Day 41. When I heard his voice I didn't get scared or cry. I told him I wished him well and that it was over. He whined a little and asked for another chance. I remember feeling sorry for his pain but I knew I wasn't the cause or the solution. On Day 41 I said "good-bye" to him and "hello" to me.

Introduction

Right Around the Bend

Welcome to the unknown. Who knows what might or might not happen over the next 40 days and 40 nights? But you've already made one sure decision, to take time out for self-discovery. With clear intention and a willingness to begin, you are certainly in for some valuable experiences, successes, lessons, and surprises.

When mountain climbers go on an excursion, they collect their gear, a compass, and a road map, and then set up a base camp to climb from. Your gear is this book and a dedication to personal growth. Your compass is your intuition, which you'll get in touch with soon enough, and your road map is your journal, which will be written as you travel. Base camp is your own home and your personal intention for the journey, which you will create momentarily. And although there is no concrete destination, the guidelines, daily activities, and journal prompts will pave the way for a satisfying and meaningful adventure.

Time Out

Based on the symbolic 40-day wanderings of the ancients and not so ancients—Jesus, Moses, Buddha, the prophets, Native Americans, and others who found clarity and purpose in the wilderness—this guided journal creates a powerful context for change. It is also a metaphor for personal transformation, from the restrictions and limitations of your current self-definition, to the expansive possibilities of who you yearn to be. Taking 40 days for self-discovery is a choice to explore who you are and who you want to become. The uncertainty of what lies ahead is balanced with the comfort of working within a finite period of time. Your excursion has a beginning, middle, and end. It is a time frame that creates a safe container for change. Although the journey might seem a bit daunting at first, the old adage "one day at a time" makes perfect sense and will keep you on track.

Why the Number 40?

Forty has been known throughout history as a mystical number. Forty days is considered a sacred period of time and is often referred to in the Bible and other ancient texts as the amount of time required for enacting change. Doing something for 40 days can make or break a habit.

The number 40 is mentioned over 120 times in the Bible. Here are just a few:

- When the Israelites were freed from slavery in Egypt, they wandered 40 years in the desert. This was seen as a time of purification and preparation for entry into the Promised Land.

- Moses was 40 years old when God called him.

- Moses went up to the summit of Mt. Sinai and spent 40 days and 40 nights. He received the first set of the Ten Commandments but the people had already created a false idol. Moses returned to Mt. Sinai for 40 more days and 40 more nights. Then he received the second set of tablets, the Ten Commandments, as we know them.

- Jesus spent 40 days and nights of solitude, prayer, and fasting in the Judean wilderness to prepare himself to do God's work.

References to the number 40 can be found in other contexts:

- In numerology, 40 symbolizes death with oneself and a spiritual rebirth. It is represented in the tarot deck as the thirteenth Hebraic letter, mem, and the Death card, marking the completion of a stage.

- According to kabbalistic writings in the Zohar, it takes 40 years to achieve the completion of a cycle of transformation, from intention to preparation to test to initiation.

- During the Renaissance, 40 days represented the complete and sufficient period to finish an important work.

- Judaism teaches that the soul enters the embryo after only 40 days.

- Legend in Jerusalem says that if you go to the Western Wall for 40 consecutive days and pray for one specific thing, it will be granted.

- According to many Eastern religions as well as the ancient Egyptians, 40 is the number of days necessary for the soul to be delivered from the body. This is why religious ceremonies to honor the dead are celebrated 40 days after a death.

- In Islam the universe is said to be supported by 40 pillars represented by the 40 columns or supports of the dome of the Mosque of Omar in Jerusalem.

- In some ancient tribes, after the circumcision, males had to withdraw themselves in the bush for a period of solitude for 40 days, at the end of which they could then return to the village.

- Buddha meditated for 40 days under the Bodhi tree. During this time, the temptations and dangers of the world threatened him, but he finally achieved enlightenment.

- The cells in your bloodstream are renewed every 40 days.

- In Kundalini Yoga, a physical and mystical program for transformation, it is said it takes 40 days to successfully drop an old habit and another 40 days for positive repatterning to set in.

As you enter into your 40 days, you will notice many activities intend to slow you down. We inhabit such a fast-paced culture that we scurry around urgently, trying to cross everything off our to-do lists. Some things, however, can be handled only with patience, intuition, and relaxation. It takes great trust and courage to slow down as you step into the unknown, but valuable learning can emerge from experiencing uncertainty.

Listen to Your Intuition

We all want answers. However, instead of going inside we often look outside and end up even more confused. Most of us fail to tap into our intuition, a key ally along the road. This formless presence, which is in, around, behind, and in between all of our thoughts, feelings, and connections to the world, is what spiritual traditions regard as our true nature. In some circles this presence is referred to as the inner witness, inner adviser, or a state of heightened awareness. During your 40 day and 40 night excursion we'll simply call it intuition. Regardless of its name or whether you are spiritually minded, religious, philosophic, psychologically bent, or just plain pragmatic, your intuition is real and it serves a valuable role.

Get Started

Inhale deeply through your nose. Hold your breath briefly. Now exhale fully out your nose and don't take another breath for three full seconds. Notice how you feel in between breaths. Do you sense the presence of something that hovers inside during this pause? When you stop doing something that is as automatic as breathing, you have the opportunity to experience a sense of heightened awareness. This naturally allows you to become aware of your intuition.

Wake Up to All of You

Although you may not be aware of it, your intuition is a feeling or voice you access all the time. It's the you that says "I want this. I don't want that," "It's time to do this," or "I don't know why, but I have a hunch about this." When you were a child it is quite possible that you asked yourself some pretty profound questions: "Who is the 'I' that I think I am?" "Why am 'I' me and not you?" Sometimes these questions were accompanied by a physical kind of sensation. Maybe you'd get a tingling on your arms, or the hair on the back of your neck would stand up, or you'd see fleeting images, or hear words and sounds. These are typical physical clues your intuition makes to get your mind's attention. As you read this ask yourself, "Who is taking in these words?" Who is experiencing all of this right now?" Without trying to think of an answer, look directly inside the part of you that is "experiencing consciousness" itself. What you'll find is something, or someone that has no shape, location, or form. No one yet knows how a human body can be home to something that is so seemingly nonphysical as intuition. However, when you learn to quiet down and stay present with yourself, you get in touch with this sixth sense that gives information beyond the obvious.

You Have Choices

This book will help you become more comfortable accessing your intuition. As you do, you'll slowly be able to step outside your daily life, and like a gentle bystander, will observe yourself. You'll begin to notice the difference between the things you want to do and the things that are no longer important or necessary. You may even notice the things that actually drive you a little nuts! As you become more agile at accessing your intuition, you'll begin to recognize you have far more options in what you think and do, and will discover more choices in all areas of your life. So, take time out from your constant efforts to control, comply, manage, rush, run, and figure it all out. Enjoy this breather, get in touch with your intuition, and open your heart and mind to something bigger.

How this book works

This book will change the way you relate to yourself and the rest of your life. It helps you dedicate a manageable but inspired time and space for conscious growth. It provides an easy to follow, step-by-step framework for succeeding on your personal quest. Before you get going, you will need to set an intention or focus for your journey—something important you want to accomplish or discover—whether ending a stagnant relationship, or changing jobs, or just giving yourself permission to read and garden more, or finding out your life's true calling.

The following section will explain how to choose your intention, but before you do that, take a moment to review how this book is organized. *40 Days and 40 Nights* consists of four thematic chapters, which are divided into 10-day segments that are designed to build upon one another. Chapter One, Stepping Out of the Everyday, prepares you for your excursion; Chapter Two, Getting Lost and Liking It, is a time of incubation, where you begin to search the depths of your past and embrace who you've been; Chapter Three, Getting Found and Waking Up, illuminates your habits and patterns and helps you make new choices; and Chapter Four, Endings and New Beginnings, encourages you to re-create yourself and your life based on what you've learned.

Each 10-day segment is filled with activities, journal prompts, blank journal sheets, and stories to keep you inspired and on track. The activities and journal prompts are tools that:

—Enhance your ability to focus and work through uncertainty

—Encourage you to slow down and listen

—Allow you to practice self-acceptance and trust

—Help you break out of patterns and activate new possibilities

—Open up your imagination

—Show you how to take what you learn into the rest of life

How Do I Begin?

Look at your calendar and plan ahead, but not too far! Know that this process will take five to 15 minutes a day, so it is do-able under most ordinary circumstances. Be sure to choose a time frame that allows you to dedicate a continuous 40 days to the process.

When, Where, and How Long?

There is no need to wander in the desert, become an ascetic, or sit in a dark cave! Take 40 days in your home or anywhere else, but it helps if you make your environment a little more conducive to the process. Here are a few things you might want to do to prepare:

- Make sure you create a space that is private and comfortable to do your daily activities and journal writing. Clear an area and make it cozy with pillows and flowers. You might want to light a candle or put on some music. Use a favorite pen, sit by a window, wear a special shawl, or sip warm tea. This is your space to define your needs—anything goes.

- Choose a time of day to do your daily explorations. Early morning is a great way to jump-start your day. However, it may be energizing to do the daily activities when you wake up and then comforting to respond to the journal prompts at night. No matter what time you choose, try not to skip a day.

- The activity and journal prompts take five to 15 minutes to complete. So, make sure you let the significant people in your life know you might disappear for a few minutes in the morning or at night.

A Little Bit About Journal Writing

The journal pages in this book are a safe place to go for daily inspiration and reflection as well as a practical way to check into what's going on. It is as if someone were waiting inside the pages, ready to listen to what happened today. As you move through your 40 days and 40 nights, you will have the chance to explore all sides of yourself—your fears, aspirations, life stories you've forgotten about, and other things you never knew you knew. Inside these pages feel free to cry, vent, laugh, and sigh. It's an easy way to get up close and personal, and you will be creating an invaluable record of your insights and heightened awareness along the way.

Something magical happens when you put pen to paper. You open up, breathe a little easier, and even find yourself being more honest and forgiving. By filling in the blanks, you will discover what's on your mind and in your heart as well as how to make your intention a reality. Since your inner life is really quite abstract, writing it down helps solidify it. You'll be able to articulate things you've never said to others or even to yourself. Unexpected insights will arise. And you'll end up with a revealing and informative record of where you've been and some clues about where you are going.

Sometimes you'll be surprised by what you write. So have courage. You'll find out the most profound journal writing comes from deep within your heart, the place where fear hides and tenderness lies.

Ten Guidelines for Journal Writing

- Write daily. That's right, 40 days in a row.

- It's okay if you don't fill in all of the blanks, but don't skip days.

- Print or write. Fast or slow.

- Write in your natural speaking voice as much as you can.

- Tell the truth. Don't edit. Don't hold back.

- Don't worry about dotting your i's or crossing your t's.

- There is no need to dress up your language or revise your first inklings.

- Modify your writing pace according to how you feel. Energetic? Write fast! More reflective? Take your time.

- Vary your writing style, too. Print in big shouting letters if you get the urge. Or make your handwriting oh so tiny and meticulous.

- Each day features an activity to try out followed by a set of journal prompts ending with the simple word "Today..." This is part of your diary, a place for you to reflect and write whatever you've noticed, need to express, or keep track of for that day.

STARBUCKS | ♪ iTunes

To download your free content on iTunes:

1. Download iTunes for Mac or Windows, free of charge at www.iTunes.com.
2. Open iTunes and click iTunes Store.
3. Click Redeem under Quick Links.
4. Enter the code on this card. Your download will start immediately. Enjoy.

The code expires on the date below and is redeemable only on the U.S. iTunes Store. To redeem the code you must have an iTunes account, subject to prior acceptance of license and usage terms. To open an account you must be above the age of 13 and in the U.S. iTunes 8.0 or later (7.0 or later for classic), compatible hardware and software, and internet access (fees may apply) are required. Not for resale. For full terms, see www.apple.com/legal/itunes/us/gifts.html. For more information, see www.apple.com/support/itunes/store.

Download Code:

J7KL6HEF7RM9

STARBUCKS | iTunes

Pick of the Week

song
DIDO
Quiet Times

Come to Starbucks
every Tuesday for
a new free pick.

Code on
back.

Choosing an Intention

This book is based on choosing an intention for the next 40 days and 40 nights—a way to align and connect with what is important to you right now. It is a personal agreement that puts an energetic *focus* on your particular vision. Intention is also about *action*, since it actively directs your attention toward self-inquiry and personal truth. A true commitment to self-inquiry combined with a solid framework of activities and reflection promotes self-knowledge and positive change.

Coming up with an intention for the next 40 days requires a commitment to honestly reflect on your current values, beliefs, behaviors, and habits. It is time to consider how you want them to change, expand, and grow. All intentions revolve around self-discovery first and foremost. However, many of you may want to address specific issues that reflect one of the following basic themes:

- Health—mental, physical, and emotional
- Love, family, relationships
- Money, career, work
- Creativity, expression, dreams
- Higher purpose, spiritual growth

Your intention can be practical

Perhaps you want to reconsider being involved in a particular relationship. Or you want to deal with your money problems. Or you want to quit a bad habit—like rushing around all the time. Or you want to stop skipping meals.

Your intention may be spiritual or philosophic

You may want to learn to really listen better. You may want to face and accept the truth and be honest with yourself. You may want to pay attention to your dreams, immerse yourself more in nature, or pray regularly.

Your intention might be vague

Even if you aren't quite sure about the specifics of your intention, choosing to take 40 days for self-discovery means you are curious about exploring time for yourself. You may wish to focus your intention on the gifts of solitude or on a specific desire to develop more self-acceptance.

As you formulate your intention, ask yourself the following four questions:

- What is it I wish to enhance?

- What is it I wish to let go of?

- What is it I wish to discover or uncover?

- What is it I wish to manifest?

Listen. Wait for an answer. Or you may already know. If you do, write down your intention here, clearly and succinctly.

_____

_____

_____

_____

_____

If you don't know what it is at the moment, review the following list. Remember, intentions come in all sizes and shapes.

Intention List

Practical

I want to read more.
Face my finances, finally.
I want to worry less. (about . . . career, the future, the past)
Spend more time with friends and loved ones.
Give up being a TV news junkie.
Learn how to spend quality time with myself.
Stop eating meat. Stop drinking. Stop smoking.
Clean up the garage.
Change jobs.
Consider moving to a new home or town.
Meditate.
Build something from scratch. Bake something from scratch.
End relationships that don't work.
Play the cello. Pick up my old instrument.
Check in with people I've lost touch with.
Go to cooking school.
Walk more.
Volunteer. Mentor. Do community service.
Devote more time to the kids.
See more art. Listen to more music. Immerse myself in culture.
Finish unfinished business. Finalize things in love and work.
Plan a big trip.
Garden more.
Change my schedule so I have more time off.
Simplify, downsize, consume less.
Less computer time and more time with friends and family.
Give things away.
Take out the telescope and look at the moon.
Pick up my paintbrush. Write a novel.
Take a long drive with no destination.

Spiritual or Philosophic

Find something to believe in.
Rediscover my faith.
Pay more attention to my dreams.
Break out of stagnant automatic living.
Discover my true values. Live by them.
Learn more about myself.
Indulge in solitude and quiet time.
Actively express and embrace love.
Be less critical of myself and others.
Find more joy.
Talk to God.
Stop rushing. Slow down. Cultivate patience.
Be less rigid.
Be less bound by the clock.
Examine my priorities.
Take more risks.
Stop holding grudges and/or resentments. Let go of regrets.
Find my "true work."
Use my imagination more.
Gain a clear idea of what legacy I may want to leave.
Consider what paths may need to be walked before I die. And
  walk them!

You also have the option of leaving your intention open. Or perhaps you wish to take your 40-day excursion as an experiment in itself, perhaps you want to celebrate a major birthday, focus on a challenging life transition, or take time out to heal from a serious crisis or trauma.

By the way, this book is not about doing penance. It is not about imposing physical hardships, tests, or harsh challenges to your beliefs. And it is not a recovery program. Although it will help you learn more about who you are and why you do what you do, it is not designed or guaranteed to help you alter serious emotional or physical problems or behaviors.

Set an Intention and Then Let It Go!

Once you choose an intention, acknowledge it and let it go. Simply drop it into your unconscious and go about living. You will notice that most days, the activities and journal prompts are *not* dedicated to helping you make your particular intention a reality. Successful change and growth is really a function of relaxing and being open. It means creating space for the new. In other words accept yourself as you are, and then creatively step into your vision. It is not about willing with all your might or working hard at anything. So simply take your intention to heart and then move through the daily activities and journal prompts—relax, write, breathe, and find your own unique way.

Ten Important Reminders

- You will not be able to predict what may or may not happen. Hooray!

- Instead of asking others for advice, seek your own counsel.

- Initially, feelings of discomfort, fear, uncertainty, and even disconnection might come up. This is a healthy sign.

- Trust yourself. Trust your instincts. Trust the process.

- Don't gossip about what goes on during your private time out.

- Every day counts. Don't skip days.

- Be aware of your intention but don't try to "work" on it. Discovery is about allowing, not trying.

- Create some additional quiet or alone time for yourself every day.

- Celebrate your commitment.

- Go all the way. This is your time!

STEPPING OUT OF THE EVERYDAY
Preparation

Learn to Relax

Remember being a kid and getting all bent out of shape over something or other? Then your grandmother or aunt told you to take a deep breath and count to 10 before you exploded? It's sound advice. Getting oxygen to the brain clears out the cobwebs and helps you relax. It's amazing what waiting a few seconds can do to alter how you face yourself and the world.

Learning how to relax over the next 40 days is the key to getting the most out of this time. When you are relaxed, you are more in touch with your inner resources of power, energy, and the ability to focus. You will find more space inside to open up to something new. As you unwind, slow down, and look around, you will have more distance from negativity and self-doubt. Every thought and emotion makes its imprint on our physical being. Many of us are physically stressed without knowing it because we mistakenly imagine our mind and body as separate. If we were more conscious of the beating our physical body takes on a daily basis from our ramped up mental and emotional lives we might try to learn to relax more often. So when your body is relaxed, there's a good chance you'll be calmer and more at ease inside and out.

Expand Your Senses and Listen

Over the next 10 days you are invited to use all of your senses more fully. Sensation is often experienced as a kaleidoscope, where each impression flashes elusively and is rarely fully absorbed. It's time to train your mind to heighten its sensual awareness. You'll spend one day focusing on each of the basic five senses: sight, taste, smell, sound, and touch. In this way you will give each sense the appreciation it deserves.

Human beings are wired to use our sight, taste, smell, sound, and touch to pull inside what's going on outside. This is how we interpret and respond to the world around us. We take in data and make daily decisions based on reading people's expressions, evaluating their tone of voice, feeling the humidity on our skin, or smelling something intoxicating or repugnant. Our senses are the way we understand reality and they let us know what is going on. Am I safe? Will it rain? Is this poisonous?

You will also learn to understand your intuition, often called the sixth sense. All of us possess this elusive ability to know or sense what is beyond our conscious, rational, or logical mind. However, most of us fail to take our intuition seriously. Our culture undervalues this hidden asset and often treats it as weird or marginal. However, our intuition is a rich database that is worth using and trusting. It is a form of protection in the biggest sense of the word, and when we begin to learn how to listen and use it effectively, our lives will reflect more of who we truly are.

Your intuition might show up in many different ways:

- A tingling in your arms

- A sensation in your gut

- A voice in your ear

- Butterflies in your stomach

- A pounding in your head

- A red light flashing
- A dizzy sensation

Over time you will learn to sort out these clues and create a more comfortable, direct line with your intuition for information and guidance.

Your Intuition

Before we can listen to our intuition we must learn how to be quiet. With the constant droning of TV, telephones, traffic, and machinery it is no wonder we are tuning out and becoming deaf, not only to what is around us, but also to what is going on inside ourselves. But many of us find being still, or even silent uncomfortable—possibly even threatening. People often punish one another with the "silent treatment." Words and noise seem to mean everything is normal. However, quiet is not the absence of sound. The inner essence of quiet feels warm and enveloping, creates breathing room, and connects us to something greater than our to-do list and the bubbling stew of chitchat and worries that tend to fill our ever-spinning minds. The next 40 days will help you quiet your chattering mind and the world around you so that you can *really* listen.

Day 1: Say "Ahhh"

This is the beginning. It's time to shift out of your normal routine and step into a softer, slower way of being.

Activity

Open up your mouth and yawn big and wide. Make full relaxing yawning sounds and say "Ahhhh" as you exhale. Let your eyes crinkle and your nose wrinkle, and even let your tongue hang out for maximum relaxation. How does yawning make you feel? Yawn as you write your first journal entries, and open up your whole body to a new beginning. Indulge in the pleasure of deep yawning throughout the day to get stale air, old thoughts, and beliefs out while pulling fresh new opportunities into your mind and oxygen into your bloodstream.

> ### More . . .
>
> *To relax more deeply, lightly press your fingertips against tight spots on your jaw and with tiny circular motions stroke away any tension. People aren't the only ones who yawn. Watch a cat or dog get ready for a nap, and you'll probably see it take a gigantic yawn as its mouth opens wide and its tongue pops out. Even unborn babies are known to yawn.*

Journal Prompts

—Write a list of your fears and anxieties (worst-case scenarios) that might come up over the next 40 days. Include all obstacles you anticipate that might bring you down or stand in your way . . .

—List the positive inklings and "good feelings" you have about what you are doing . . .

—Today . . .

Day 2: Shadow Play

Take time to be alone with the magic of the moment. Where does a shadow begin and end? It only takes attention and the willingness to see to fully appreciate something.

Activity

Stare at a shadow or reflection cast from the sun or artificial light source. It is not easy to focus on something that amorphous and vague. Blink as little as possible. Soften your eyes. Describe what you see.

More . . .

Seventy percent of the body's sense receptors cluster in the eyes. It is mainly through seeing the world that we size it up and understand it. Yet there is so much more to life than meets the eye!

Journal Prompts

—List the big and small surprises that have happened to you. Were any life changing?

—What do you like to do when you are alone? Does being alone make you feel like something is right or wrong? Why?

—Today . . .

Day 3: Soft Eyes

Nature is a powerful force that is capable of showering you with beauty and joy if you just take a peek and soak it in.

Activity

Wander around outside and with soft, unfocused eyes make a 360-degree circular scan of your surroundings. If you are an urban dweller, seek out a semi-secluded park. Soft eyes allow what is "out" there to find *you* instead. Without looking for anything in particular, let the world fill up your field of vision. Now close your eyes and choose something you noticed in passing, be it a cloud, a lawn chair, or a bug. Describe it from memory.

_____

_____

_____

_____

_____

_____

More . . .

Astronomers often use what is called averted vision to "see" faint objects in the night sky. Instead of observing something straight on, this technique encourages looking off to the side, which allows more light to fall on the sensitive periphery of the retina in the eye. Seen straight on, many stars appear as vague glowing clouds. Averted vision reveals these clouds as very individual specks with unique forms and diverse origins.

Journal Prompts

—What would you do if you had more free time?

—What important activities, chores, trips, or creations have you been putting on hold? Do you think you'll ever get around to doing these things?

—List the wild or forbidden activities that call to you—from swimming naked to jumping out of airplanes, to eating all the chocolate you crave.

—Today . . .

Day 4: Eavesdrop

The world is loud. There's nature, machines, technology, and our own internal chatter. We get used to hearing all this noise and eventually tune out even what really matters.

Activity

Pretend your ear is a giant receiver. Now wander around your home, preferably at night, and listen. Stop, turn your head left and right for better reception. Are clocks ticking, washing machines rumbling, sirens wailing, boom boxes thumping? Stick your ear out the door and listen. What do you hear? Which sounds are appealing? Which irritate you? Why?

More . . .

Sound *comes from "gesund," meaning unbroken, thorough, and healthy. Think "sound mind and body." Sound also means being trustworthy and stable. We rely on the buzz of the alarm to get us up on time. We respond to invasive sounds that don't sound like they belong in our environment—like footsteps or sirens—to alert us and keep us safe.*

Journal Prompts

—Dip into your memory bank and write about the sounds of familiar voices. What words were spoken at your front door or in the bedroom? Arguments or tears? Be as specific as possible.

—Think about the times you were truly heard. Who truly listened? How did it feel?

—Today . . .

Day 5: Soft Belly

When you loosen all the tension and worry in your body you will discover a fresh, undistorted, juicy you!

Activity

Sit comfortably with both feet on the floor. Put your hands on your belly and feel it pulling away from your body as you inhale. Imagine you are gently filling up a balloon inside your belly. Hold your breath for three full seconds. Now exhale softly out of your mouth deflating this imaginary balloon for five full seconds. Let the muscles of the belly soften.

More . . .

Encouraging a soft belly is a natural way to eliminate stress. We spend so much time holding everything in. This body and mind tightness uses up a lot of energy and actually restricts blood flow. Warm up your inner self by softening your middle. Your breathing will become fuller, you will relax, and almost automatically a feeling of safety and satisfaction will wash over you.

Journal Prompts

—List what you are postponing because it is too scary, too difficult, or too painful . . .

—List your regrets, disappointments, your most profound "If onlys . . ." and "I should haves." Choose one and pretend you have the power to change the past. How would your life be different right now?

—Today . . .

Quick Check-In:

How are you doing? What is happening to your commitment to your intention? Are you worried about it? Is your intention changing? Are you? How?

_____

_____

_____

_____

_____

_____

_____

_____

_____

_____

_____

_____

_____

_____

_____

_____

Day 6: Count Down and Slow Down

Slowing down is a skill that cultivates and promotes patience, relaxation, and a deeper connection to your intuition.

Activity

Lie on your back with arms and legs spread comfortably apart. Imagine you are sinking down into warm sand. Close your eyes and notice where you hold tension. Breathe slowly and count silently from 40 to zero. Synchronize your breathing with your counting. Inhale and then silently count 40 on your exhale. Inhale and count 39 on your exhale. Remember, let the breath lead the count and not the other way round. Don't rush. When you get to zero melt deeper into the sand, whisper, and repeat, "I welcome the unknown. I trust in myself and in this time."

> ### More . . .
>
> *There is an old Polish saying: "Sleep faster, we need the pillows."*
> *It reminds us that there are some activities that will simply not be rushed. Remember, if you start tugging on a fishing line, the knot just becomes tighter.*

Journal Prompts

—Who and what do you love? Include everything from people and places to objects, songs, and movies.

—What does heaven look like? What happens after you die? Paint a word picture of what you truly believe.

—Today . . .

Day 7: Listen to Your Heart

The Chinese verb "to listen" contains the characters signifying "heart," "ears," "eyes," "undivided attention," and "you." That's really listening!

Activity

Place the fingers of your dominant hand on the opposite wrist by wrapping your index, third, and fourth fingers gently around the back of your wrist. Using light pressure, allow your fingertips to make contact with your pulse. Do not use your thumb. Make contact with your heartbeat and close your eyes. Silently listen and feel the rhythm of your own heartbeat.

More . . .

In ancient Chinese calligraphy, the symbol for mind and the symbol for heart are the same—Hsin. It is thought that when the mind is unclouded only heart is experienced. Just as when heart is exposed there are no obstacles in the mind. The heart and mind only seem separate to the mind. To the heart, they are one.

Journal Prompts

—How does your intuition speak to you? List some hunches you've actually followed. What happened?

—List the times you chose not to trust your instincts. Why didn't you? What happened?

—Today . . .

Day 8: Ask for Guidance

It is time to suspend judgment and ask for guidance. Open a line of communication between you and your intuition and listen with the intent to really hear.

Activity

Calm down and relax. Put fingertips to pulse again. Find your heartbeat, release, and sit quietly. Then whisper the following words: "What do I need to know to help me with my intention? What do I need to do or not do?" Let things percolate. Listen for your intuition—it might be a voice, a body sensation, or fleeting images. Write down whatever comes to you; it's almost like taking dictation.

_____

_____

_____

_____

_____

_____

More . . .

Remember the childhood game called "telephone"? You sat in a circle and whispered a complete sentence into the ear of the child next to you. And he'd whisper it into the ear of the child next to him. By the time the words got back to the original speaker and were spoken aloud it was always hilariously garbled and twisted! You can only imagine what happens when you don't listen clearly to your own thoughts!

Journal Prompts

—Whose voice do you love the sound of? Why? How does it affect you?

—Write down a secret you've kept a long time. How does it feel to finally spill it out?

—Today . . .

_____

_____

_____

_____

_____

_____

_____

_____

_____

_____

_____

_____

_____

_____

_____

_____

_____

_____

_____

DAY 9: FLOATING EYES

As we dash from task to task our eyes perpetually pull us forward. Give your eyes and mind a relaxing break.

Activity

Look at your index finger, touch your nose, and cross your eyes. Do it twice. On the third time close your eyes and encourage them to float gently upward. It feels good. Gaze at the spot between your eyebrows. What sensation do you feel? Over time, this becomes very relaxing.

More . . .

In yoga, the space between the eyebrows is called the Third Eye and was said to be the center of our intuition. This area actually covers the front of the skull and brain that houses the pituitary gland. This master gland makes and regulates serotonin production, the so-called "feel-good" brain enzyme.

Journal Prompts

—What would today look like if everything went "right"?

—It is your last day on planet Earth. What would you like to do?

—Today . . .

DAY 10: SAVOR THE SWEETNESS

Chewing is so primal and satisfying. We rarely taste the true sweetness of food because we don't take the time.

Activity

Put one raisin or tiny piece of fruit or chewy bread into your mouth. Stop before you automatically swallow and reach for the next morsel! Then roll it around on your tongue and feel its texture. Now chew ever so slowly. Notice how a rich sweetness seeps out and fills your mouth with flavor. Savor the taste and do not hurry to swallow. This is difficult because we are not accustomed to being nourished by food in this manner—but try it anyway.

More . . .

Tastes and smells can soothe and excite. A fragrance enters your nose with little interference and goes straight to the limbic system in your brain. That's the ancient center of emotion and creativity that houses inklings for lust, longing, and an entire palette of human feelings. Chewing is so deeply satisfying that when surveyed, people over 80 said they missed the pleasurable sensation of chewing bread, crisp apples, licorice, and peanuts.

Journal Prompts

—List the smells you love and dislike from the past and the memories they elicit.

—List all the foods you love to eat.

—Today . . .

CHECKING IN:

- Reflect on and review days 1–10. Make a list of three things you have learned about yourself. Make a list of three questions you wonder about.

- How has this piece of time inspired or informed your intention?

_____

_____

_____

_____

_____

_____

_____

_____

_____

_____

_____

_____

_____

_____

GETTING LOST AND LIKING IT
Incubation

Limbo and Uncertainty

Congratulations. You have really stepped inside your self and this book! But are you having fun yet? When you stop doing what you are used to doing or when you introduce a new set of behaviors you often don't feel quite like yourself. You may feel out of sorts, tired, anxious, or even lost. That's normal. As you question or move away from your deeply ingrained routines, life might start looking a little darker, more chaotic, or a little cloudy. This is not the end. It is a state of limbo and you may find yourself temporarily in between "here and there." This is a state of incubation and it's just right—for now.

Days 11–21 are dedicated not only to helping you tell the truth to yourself and dive deeper into the true you, but also to hang on through the necessary discomfort of growing pains. This is a time to be daring, in a less obvious way. It is time to practice brutal honesty, a time to search the emotional depths of your being, and foster faith in the process. Be patient with your uncertainty and acquiesce to the unknown. This may sound puzzling, but it is useful to learn to function—even shine—in this place.

Self-Criticism and Self-Acceptance

If you really look at what contributes to the problems and discomforts that surround you, you'll see that liberal layers of guilt and self-recrimination, dollops of righteous indignation, and scoops of anger abound. You'll find fault with parts of yourself and get stuck inside the sticky drama of your life, but self-acceptance and forgiveness are the true way out. Because if you can't accept yourself, you can't really let go of yourself! This is not always easy, since self-doubt begins early. When you were young, did you ever have stomachaches or vague feelings something wasn't quite right? When you mentioned it to your parents or elders, did they say you were imagining things? As you grow older, you may end up suspecting your own instincts and your memory as well. Remember, *your* version is *your* version. Ignore past influences. You are entitled to your feelings and your response to life as it presents itself. It's time to learn to trust yourself and all of your feelings.

But most of us deny the parts of ourselves we deem unacceptable. Until we truly own the rejected parts of ourselves we suffer and become trapped in projecting them onto others. When we bring all of our selves into the fold, something amazing happens. Along with the parts we don't like, a lot of the parts we do like show up stronger. Don't forget, it takes sand to create a pearl. All of our forbidden faces—all of the ones we hide from ourself and the world—have more to offer us than shame. They are the parts that will ultimately help us understand ourselves better. You see, when you transform your inner world, your outer world is transformed as well.

Day 11: Under the Rug

Most of us keep our dark side hidden. Hiding from these seemingly defective pieces actually stunts our growth. Facing the good, the bad, and the ugly actually releases pent-up energy and fosters self-love.

Activity

Everybody has a junk drawer, overstuffed garage, or cluttered closet. Locate that one really messy place and look inside. What do you find? What purpose is it serving? Why can't you throw this stuff out? Is there anything precious you've overlooked?

> *More . . .*
>
> *Odysseus was described as intellectually brilliant. But like everyone else, he was somewhat ignorant about his own nature. For 10 years he wandered at sea and then finally returned home, a new man. It seems in all mythology and religion that in order for individuals to become strong enough to create cosmos (or their own reality) each needs a certain amount of chaos. It's a necessary step in the movement into conscious creation.*

Journal Prompts

—Who has called you the most critical and dismissive names, and what were they?

—Who are you totally yourself with? Why?

—Today . . .

Day 12: Eye to I

It is said that the touch of a hand, a word spoken, and eye contact open the heart more than all the knowledge and mystical practices in the world.

Activity

Gaze at yourself in the bathroom mirror. Stand quietly and really look—first in one eye and then the other. Whisper, "Who am I?" over and over until you see into both eyes at once. What comes up? Do you look away? Are you immediately drawn into self-criticism? Who is looking back at you? Is this difficult? Do this once a day and notice how quickly you begin to meet yourself in new and surprising ways.

More . . .

Reality is layered, like an onion. Asking questions is one of the ways you can peel off the layers one by one, to find out what is now really real for you. Asking, "Who am I?" will de-solidify your identity. For a split second, you may actually feel yourself leave your body only to return to make a new connection. Questioning draws out your truth. Revelation is part of the payoff. So never trade a good question for an answer.

Journal Prompts

—Sign your name over and over again. Fill one entire page.

—Record the words that define who you are and who you've been . . .
  (female, short, funny, a parent, a teacher, brunette, unitarian, liberal, etc.)

—Today . . .

Quick Check-In:

How are you doing? What is happening to your commitment to your intention? Are you worried about it? Is your intention changing? Are you? How?

_____

_____

_____

_____

_____

_____

_____

_____

_____

_____

_____

_____

_____

_____

_____

DAY 13: A E I O U

Sound opens up your throat, warms your face, massages your heart, and uplifts your spirit. The most vital piece of your acoustic environment is the human voice.

Activity

Place your hands on your breastbone and sing or chant the vowels A E I O U over and over again. Close your eyes and feel the vibration until the individual letters melt into a bed of calming reverberation. When you run out of breath, bathe in the silence and repeat. Then cup your hands over your ears with a mild suction and make the sound "Mmmmmmmmmmm." You can feel the soothing resonance.

More . . .

Many animals, including birds, fish, and lizards, camouflage themselves so successfully they seem to disappear. Ancient yogis claimed they had the power to disappear as well. Remember the Cheshire Cat? He would engage in a curious conversation and then vanish slowly from tail to head, leaving only a toothy grin.

Journal Prompts

—List all of your positive character traits.

—How do you disappear? How do you check out?

—Finish the following sentence: "If I ever let myself completely go . . ." What might happen?

—Today . . .

DAY 14: IN THE DARK

Awareness is like a beam of light. Until you shine your inner light on what's going on inside, you may feel lost, confused, and in the dark.

Activity

Tonight, go into your bedroom and sit on your bed in the dark. Don't close your eyes, but soak in the darkness. (If you wear glasses, take them off.) Just do nothing. Encourage yourself to spend a longer time in this usually familiar place. You may get bored, uncomfortable, or impatient. Count the times you want to get up or turn on the light. Notice what happens. Being in the dark makes us vulnerable but it also brings awareness. Pay attention and write down what you are thinking about.

> *More . . .*
>
> *The average eye blinks about once every five seconds, or 17,000 times each day, or 6¼ million times a year! When in a darkened room, the eye muscles are encouraged to relax. Upon leaving the dark, many people who wear glasses discover less tension in their eyes and once in the light actually notice temporarily improved vision.*

Journal Prompts

—Were you ever afraid of the dark? Were you ever afraid of the boogeyman or whatever lay under your bed or hid in your closet?

—How have you come back from despair, trauma, heartache, or disappointment? What did you do to break out of the darkness?

—Today . . .

Day 15: Rant and Rave

We edit so much of what we need to say because we want to behave properly. Trying to be nice all the time hurts and stifles you.

Activity

Are you angry, furious, or full of rage? What triggers your anger? Rant, rave, and get it off your chest. Been dumped, lied to, or cheated on? Let your voice be heard. Spit out all the things you want to say to whomever did you wrong. Shout out loud! Try it when you are in your car, or home alone. Give it all you've got. How about a booming "Get out of my life." Or "I've had it. No more." Vocalize what you need to say and be done with it.

> ### More . . .
> *The tongue is the strongest muscle in the human body, but unlike the other 700 or so other muscles, the tongue does not produce much lactic acid when it works too hard. That means it won't get stiff or sore when you use it. Speaking, singing, and screaming use the tongue muscle equally.*

Journal Prompts

—List all of the people from your life, past and present, who push your emotional buttons or drive you crazy . . .

—What is going on right now that breaks your heart, makes you angry, or makes you feel powerless?

—Today . . .

Day 16: Self-Forgiveness

You don't need to fix yourself. Just relax without moralizing or harshness. Accept and applaud all of who you are.

Activity

Take the following meditation of friendliness and self-love to heart. Repeat throughout the days to come: "I accept all of who I am, who I was, who I ever will become."

More . . .

There are hundreds of psychological filters that can dramatically distort your listening. There's the "I only want to listen to spiritual things . . ." filter, and the "I only want to hear happy things" filter. Take an inventory of your filters so that as you begin to listen to all of the rattles in your head you can sort through the noise and expectations and get to the gold.

Journal Prompts

—Make a list of qualities you admire in other people including your family, friends, and public and fictional heroes.

—How do you know when someone loves you? How do you know when you love someone?

—Today . . .

Day 17: Risk Telling the Truth

We are trained to lie, not openly, of course. Eventually we learn to say what people want to hear and we act accordingly. How can this help support understanding or intimacy?

Activity

Choose someone and tell him or her the whole truth and nothing but the truth. It could be your spouse, your boss, or a relative. Make a special time and place and do it. Jot down what happened that you might not have expected.

_____

_____

_____

_____

_____

More . . .

Telling the truth creates a chemical change in the body. After the initial adrenal rush that comes with fear and facing the unknown, the body goes through a form of release that is obvious and physical. Endorphins flood the system, promoting a feeling of relief and well-being.

Journal Prompts

—What if someone finds this journal? How would you feel?

—List the people you need and the people who need you . . .

—Today . . .

DAY 18: LESS IS MORE

A simple way to reinvent yourself is to stop and interrupt your normal daily routine. You may find you live more when you do less.

Activity

Today, notice what you do that drains your energy—physical, mental, or emotional. Immediately STOP and ask yourself: Why am I doing this? Is this really what *I* want or need to do? Stand up and shout "No!" 10 times in a row. Remember, when you say "no" it is like saying "yes" to yourself.

> *More . . .*
>
> *Sticking out your tongue is a way to deal with social interactions that you don't like. It comes from your infant years when you didn't know how to say "no" and so instead displayed your tongue. Saying "no" out loud is actually a highly evolved form of being able to reject something without having to act it out.*

Journal Prompts

—List some incidences when you said "yes" instead of "no" and what the outcome was.

—Why do you do things that aren't what you really want or need?

—Today . . .

DAY 19: HEAD TO GROUND

The tribulations that we endure test our patience and faith. Bowing is a way to humble ourselves before the grandeur and the mystery of life.

Activity

Kneel on the ground and sit back on your heels. Keeping your buttocks down and your palms on the ground beside your knees, bow forward slowly and touch the earth with your forehead. Linger with eyes closed and breathe.

More . . .

Bowing is a way of honoring and thanking something larger than we are. It is a way to kiss the earth. It creates a sense of safety and has been proven to slow down the heartbeat. It is satisfying to surrender and humble ourselves as we acknowledge the many gifts that make our lives rich.

Journal Prompts

—List all of the illnesses, accidents, and tragedies that you have survived.

—List all the things you have to feel grateful for.

—Today . . .

Day 20: Inner Cocktail Party

We are often defensive about what goes on inside of us. Your inner world, however, colors how you feel, behave, and the choices you make. Sometimes it might even sound like a cocktail party inside!

Activity

Sometime today you will face a decision. Large or small, there's a good chance you'll hear different voices in your head vying for attention. Instead of deciding who is "right" or "wrong," listen to everybody. Then make a list and name the key players. There's usually a loudmouthed critic, a worrywart, the voice of a parent, and the "you never listen to me" voice.

_____

_____

_____

_____

_____

_____

More . . .

Life is a dance of opposites. To be in touch with all sides requires the courage and acceptance of all of who we are. The best and so-called worst qualities of our character live side by side. But the shadow energy, usually the hidden dark parts of our self, may not be that pleasant. To be whole and to cultivate self-love we cannot deny their existence.

Journal Prompts

—Do you feel something good is missing from your life? Did you ever
have it? If so, when did you lose it? What happened?

—What conversations or tape loops of self-doubt do you replay over and
over again in your noisy mind?

—Today . . .

CHECKING IN:

- Reflect back on your journal from days 11–20. Make a list of three things you have learned about yourself. Make a list of three questions you wonder about.

- How has this piece of time inspired or informed your intention?

_____

_____

_____

_____

_____

_____

_____

_____

_____

_____

_____

_____

_____

_____

_____

_____

GETTING FOUND AND WAKING UP
Illumination

Creatures of Habit

It is said, first you make habits, then your habits make you. Humans are truly creatures of habit. We invent our day and before we know it slip into a pattern that feels comfortable, maybe a little too comfortable. Then, we fall into the inevitable numb zone of habit and feel depressed, uninspired, or tired. We look at our work or relationships and become stagnant or bored. We're quickly going nowhere, fast.

It's important to develop rituals to make life flow. But when routines turn into ruts, we need help getting out. Although there are infinite solutions, from therapy to changing jobs, from medication to marriage, sometimes the smallest and simplest changes can catalyze profound shifts.

Imagine your usual morning routine—washing your face, combing your hair, and brushing your teeth. Suppose you take your toothbrush and use it with your nondominant hand. Up and down, and side to side. Wow, you feel so awkward and the room starts to look a little different. After criticizing your skill level, you may begin to laugh. Something is changing. What does that feel like? Sure, you might feel some discomfort, but you are also learning how to become free of habit.

Life in Review and New Choices

This chapter is devoted to turning the next 10 days upside down. You will review your life and look at it with a new set of eyes and ears. You'll

139

step back and then have the freedom to choose how you want to be. It is a chance to turn off the automatic pilot and untie the invisible threads of habit that wind through the 24-hour cycles of our lives. Routines are not just external. How we think and feel becomes habitual as well. We decide love means one thing, success and failure another, and we build our lives around matching our thoughts to what we define as reality. That's why our lives often seem so repetitive. Same thoughts, same problems. Breaking out of the prison of familiarity requires disruption, but it's well worth it.

Remember, if you do the same thing over and over again and expect different results, it certainly will not happen! So do something new. Cut your hair, or grow it. Walk to the office instead of driving. Eat ice cream for breakfast or wear purple socks to bed. If you always read the newspaper, don't. Quit wearing high heels, stop swearing, or stop rushing. Minor shifts in the steps or timing of a dance change it radically. New choices in behavior lead to big results.

Meaningful Coincidence

This chapter is also dedicated to giving you room to notice synchronicity, that is, meaningful coincidences that pop up every day. Being busy limits our ability to see connections and life often looks haphazard or random. But if you pay attention, what appears to be random merges into a pattern over time. Coincidence connects the dots and creates meaning—a story, or a feeling of belonging in your life. However, most of us discount these blips on our inner radar screens. Since we don't trust what we see, we don't notice it. When you break a habit there is space for something else, and perhaps even something better to show up!

Day 21: Linger Awhile

Your weekly schedule is an asset but also your biggest defense. Disrupt your routine a little and see what happens.

Activity

Include "linger" on today's to-do list. Schedule a trip to a place you would love to explore but never had the time or opportunity to visit. Go to an art store or wander through an aisle at your local bookstore. Consider the possibilities.

> ### More . . .
>
> *There is an old Spanish proverb that says, "Habits at first are like silken threads. Then they become cables and run our lives."*

Journal Prompts

—What is your typical morning ritual?

—Record one thing you did yesterday that might be called "out of the ordinary" . . .

—What new thing would you love to include today?

—Today . . .

Day 22: Take Off Your Wristwatch

Most of us glance at a clock and a wristwatch all day long. It's automatic. How do your habits run your life?

Activity

Today, take off your watch and cover your clocks. Granted, this isn't always possible, but give it a shot. Or consider choosing another habit to break: Don't talk on the telephone. Don't wear a necktie. Don't look in the mirror. Drive to work via a different route. Sleep in a different room. Move the furniture around. Take a bath at noon.

> ### More . . .
>
> *The first things children naturally draw on their own are trees, houses, and people. The first things children are taught to draw, besides the alphabet, are clocks. By the time they are 10 years of age children have drawn hundreds of clocks as they learn to tell time; one of the top three things kids want for Christmas are not video games and bicycles, but kid-size wristwatches!*

Journal Prompts

—Which daily habit do you identify with the most?

—Break one habit for a day and describe what happens.

—Today . . .

DAY 23: TRACK YOUR CHATTERING MIND

It is estimated the average person has about 50,000 thoughts a day! Our minds habitually dash from one thought to another, often dwelling on the past, the future, and the negative. When will it ever cease?

Activity

Sit outside in a public place, perhaps a mall or park. Watch the world go by and as you do, jot down little snippets of mind chatter. Afterward, label each with one of your typical states of mind such as: judging, desiring, disliking; thinking the worst, angry, anxious, worried; impatient, creating problems.

More . . .

The smallest task can be a form of celebration—an opportunity for heightened mindfulness, introspection, and a chance to move beyond your limitations.

Journal Prompts

—Write down all of your fears, insecurities, and worries about love, happiness, and money.

—Do you believe love is something you deserve? Do you believe happiness is something unattainable? Do you believe people with money are superficial? Why?

—Today . . .

Quick Check-In:

How are you doing? What is happening to your commitment to your intention? Are you worried about it? Is your intention changing? Are you? How?

_____

_____

_____

_____

_____

_____

_____

_____

_____

_____

_____

_____

_____

_____

_____

DAY 24: REJOICE IN THE ORDINARY

Paying attention to ordinary things is a way to express appreciation for being alive. What happens when you stop hurrying, let go of expectations, and simply immerse in the moment?

Activity

Reach in the back of the cupboard and reconnect with something you own but rarely use. Take out your good silverware, china, tablecloth, and napkins, and set the table for a meal. Take your time as you engage in ordinary daily tasks and activities, whether you are mowing the lawn, gazing out the window, or making your bed.

More . . .

In Aesop's fable about the tortoise and the hare, we see how the slow and steady progress of the tortoise made him a victor in his race against the apparently faster hare. Did the tortoise stop and smell the roses? Who knows, but slower ways of doing and being have great value.

Journal Prompts

—List the fleeting ordinary moments, conversations, and activities that bring you daily delight.

—List all of the nicknames you've been called. What is the story and meaning behind your given name? What would you like to be called?

—Today . . .

Day 25: Lighten Up

Humans are pack rats. What clutters up your life and mind that you just don't need anymore? Face the music and leave the baggage behind.

Activity

Imagine you have a gigantic empty suitcase. Fill it up with your baggage. What would that be? Throw in feelings like pride and resentment along with those old piles of magazines and clothing from the back of the closet. This is no time for self-deception. What isn't necessary? Clean off everything, including old worn-out beliefs and all the stuff hidden under your bed.

> *More . . .*
>
> *It is said the average three-bedroom home has over 350,000 things in it! And half of the population admits they are hoarders and find it emotionally painful to throw stuff out, even stuff that is broken—from snapped rubber bands to burnt-out light bulbs!*

Journal Prompts

—Who are the people in your life you would like to weed out?

—What are the things you simply can't part with just yet and why?

—Today . . .

Day 26: Keep a Line Open

Take a thoughtful pause before jumping into action and open up a direct line to your intuition. Daily tasks are great ways to practice listening. Be patient. It takes a while to hear clearly.

Activity

Before you reach for your usual CD, pause and ask yourself, out loud: "What should I play?" Listen with open ears and an open heart. Wait. Trust what you hear. Do the same thing when you are shopping for groceries or deciding the best route to the beach.

> *More . . .*
>
> *The world unfolds as you slide out of a pattern. It is like cleaning a pair of dirty old sunglasses and taking a peek at new vistas.*

Journal Prompts

—Does your intuition show up as words, a body sensation, fleeting images, or a more abstract inkling?

—Has your intuition thrown you any curves or surprise responses lately? What were they?

—Today . . .

Day 27: Personal Treasures

Memory is plastic. It creates and re-creates itself. It is similar to a muscle—when flexed it gets stronger and better at retrieving the past.

Activity

Find your box of mementos and excavate sentimental letters, photographs, pressed flowers, or ticket stubs. Explore the remnants of your past and identify the specific treasures you still hold dear.

More . . .

In the early part of the 19th century, public speakers had no teleprompters or cue cards to help as they made their speeches. As a memory aid, they would write informal notes on their shirt cuffs, and so the idiom cliché "off-the-cuff" was coined.

Journal Prompts

—Describe your first car, first kiss, first drink, first dive off a diving board, or your first pet.

—If you could salvage only one item from your personal treasures, what would it be and why?

—Today . . .

Day 28: Talk to the Rocks

Throw logic out the door and check into your imagination.

Activity

Think about the character qualities you want to develop. Maybe it is balance, maybe it is strength. Go outside and talk to a willow tree. "I need to be balanced like you. How?" Or pick up a rock, feel its warmth and weight, and talk to it. "I need my foundation strengthened. What should I do?" This sounds a little crazy, and it is. Have an entire conversation out loud. Be playful, and then write down what you imagine the tree and the rock might say.

> ## More . . .
>
> *Ancient masters taught their students philosophy by using paradoxes. The unexpected—combinations that made no sense—opened up the students' minds to new ideas and profound understandings of deep forces and unseen interconnections. Consider an old Yiddish proverb: "What's the heaviest thing in the world? An empty pocket."*

Journal Prompts

—If you could talk with anyone, alive or deceased, who would you choose and what would you want to know?

—Describe a special object, ornament, or talisman you keep nearby to give you strength or inspiration.

—Today . . .

Day 29: Slow Motion

Stretch out time. Soak in the details of daily activities and notice what usually passes you by.

Activity

Tonight, open a wine bottle with a corkscrew or a can of soup with a manual can opener. But this time, slow down your typical motions and notice the intricacy and agility of your hands manipulating a gadget you typically take for granted. Be amazed at how many things you do in a day that actually require this kind of precision but have an intrinsic beauty all their own. Or if you wish, sew a button on a blouse, trim your fingernails with a clipper, or cut flowers and arrange them in a vase.

More . . .

Throughout time, hands have been considered the direct link to our souls. Palm readers are convinced our past and future are etched in our hands. The hand is also called the heart's landscape. With more than two dozen intricate bones, it is precise and agile, filled with the ability to do everything from the mundane to the sublime. Hands type, fold, dig, caress, pull, massage, express, and tickle. They dial a phone, console a loved one, tie our shoes, and make dinner. When we're lucky, we hold someone else's hand and create a nonverbal bridge of sensation and communication.

Journal Prompts

—List the many things you do regularly on automatic pilot.

—Describe your hands. Then create a hand inventory by listing the hands you've held, and the things you do well with yours.

—Today . . .

Day 30: Cultivate Coincidence

Things don't always go the way we plan, and that's often good news. A hunch compels you to put an old business card on your desk, then someone calls, and they need that exact phone number!

Activity

Clip articles from the newspaper or tear images from magazines that appeal to you. Go through your desk drawer and salvage odds and ends. Put these things together and see what they spell out. A hidden desire? A release from the past? A clue to something hidden? Something only you know the answer to?

More . . .

Goosebumps are the result of the central nervous system sending signals out in times of fear, cold, or when certain types of emotional reactions happen—including the illogical serendipity of coincidence. Tiny muscles attached to each hair follicle constrict and suddenly make our hair stand up. This activity produces more heat, raises body temperature, and forces our minds to notice that something important has taken place.

Journal Prompts

—What serendipitous events have happened in the last few months?

—Describe in detail how you met one of your closest friends or lovers.

—Today . . .

CHECKING IN:

- Reflect back on your journal from days 21–30. Make a list of three things you have learned about yourself. Make a list of three questions you wonder about.

- How has this piece of time inspired or informed your intention?

_____

_____

_____

_____

_____

_____

_____

_____

_____

_____

_____

_____

_____

_____

ENDINGS AND NEW BEGINNINGS
Re-Creation

Playtime

It's Day 31. You've relinquished some control of your regular routine and are probably a little more comfortable inhabiting a place where things don't have to make sense all the time. Inside this ephemeral world of exploration and freedom you can reconnect with, and cultivate a sense of curiosity and play. You can step forward now without having to know where you are going, trusting in yourself and the process.

Remember sitting on the floor and creating an entire world with your toys? There was no script, no how-to manual. You made up the rules and you told the story. But where did that information come from? All mammals thrive, live, learn, and love from play. From the moment we were born, we were all eyes and ears. Curious beings, we embraced all stimulation to learn about ourselves and the world. Once we could crawl, we got to actively explore. Movement is such a huge part of the puzzle. The kinesthetics of living inform us how we think, know, and feel.

Endings and New Beginnings . . .

Life builds form constantly; we are always changing shape. But most of us don't recognize those changes and instead see ourselves in static images or roles. We remain tied, gagged, and bound to our habitual identities when we really need to say good-bye to some of the old ways. Saying good-bye is not forgetting, saying good-bye is not denying pleasure or pain. You are simply saying good-bye to patterns that are no longer usefu. But it is still "good" bye with gratitude for what was.

And of course, it's time for a new hello. Now that you have created some room to look around, you can reconnect with the rhythm of living. Instead of repeating limited behaviors that hold you down, you can now respond in more creative ways—to live and love more fully. This commit ment involves great respect for yourself and the mystery that is life. It's time to re-create yourself anew and it all comes down to courting your playful spirit.

It's time to reconnect with the place where we all love to scribble, blow soap bubbles, whistle through a blade of grass, listen to crickets, and watch the stars. Moving into play is a less tangible and more allusive way of being. There's room for mystery, abstraction, and ingenuity. It isn't jus about "fun" either. It's all about making connections between the intuitiv and the logical—between logic and truth—between what you know and what you feel. That's really the payoff of this entire excursion. Play can be a factory of knowledge. When we discover a playful solution, we arrive at a answer and can come up with another question. More questions feed self inquiry and keep us alive. This is your destination—a continued journey into self-knowledge.

DAY 31: INDULGE YOURSELF

Humans seem to build boxes around themselves, and self-imposed restrictions abound. It's time to give yourself permission to step outside you own boundaries to see what you are missing.

Activity

Today, indulge. What are you craving? What pleasure do you seek? Jump on the urge. Get in the car and just drive. Buy something expensive, or eat a hot fudge sundae. Come up with a list of indulgences and check off at least two.

More . . .

Before 1900, dry cereal had not been invented. When cereal became a commodity, however, doctors were suddenly bombarded by an endless stream of patients with stomach problems. Who could imagine a bowl of cornflakes and milk would be an enticing indulgence?

Journal Prompts

—List all of your most pleasurable and passionate experiences. Include details.

—What restrictions do you impose on yourself that are really not necessary? Why?

—Today . . .

Day 32: Shake It Up

Shaking is a natural way to let go of fear and stress. Ducks shake their feathers and bears shake their fur. Hanging loose thaws our tension and melts our mental constriction. Humans are meant to process life, not keep it frozen.

Activity

Stand with your feet shoulder width apart, arms hanging loosely at your sides. Now gently bounce and get really loose. Let your arms dangle, your neck bop, your shoulders float up and down. Open your mouth and let some sounds escape. Keep it moving, loosen up your skin, make a face, but keep your feet on the floor as you increase speed and intensity. Shake it up and relax!

More . . .

The largest and heaviest human organ is the skin. It is literally our birthday suit, with a total surface area of about 20 square feet for the average person. It is easy to energize and stimulate the entire body by massaging or manipulating the skin. It responds in kind by ramping up its ability to deliver nutrients and oxygen to the entire body, while cleaning house at the same time.

Journal Prompts

—Describe a time you were lost on a hike, in the forest, or on the road. How did you find your way back?

—What are some things that restore you and give you peace of mind?

—Today . . .

Day 33: Monkey Around

When we play we automatically access novelty, stimulation, and adventure without even having to leave the house.

Activity

Pretend you are an animal, an insect, or a plant. Close your eyes and mimic its appearance, sounds, and movements. How might you take some of its attractive or unique behavior into your own life?

More . . .

Playing means you do a simple activity with no demands. You get lost in discovery. You just enjoy yourself and forget what time it is.

Journal Prompts

—List where you would go if you could go anywhere in the world. Who would you take with you?

—What are your best memories of childhood fun?

—Today . . .

Day 34: No More Frogs, Bats, and Squirrels

It has been said that life is learning how to lose gracefully, and yet we all struggle so hard against life's losses. Growing beyond our own pain helps us open up our hearts.

Activity

Curl up in a fetal position in a very private place. Close your eyes and focus on your own cries of indignation, sorrow, and yearning. You'll find yourself lighter and more at ease. Then drop your own personal story and move beyond yourself. Pour out unconditional compassion for the entire world's sadness by whispering a chant of goodwill and faith. May all of us be happy and free from suffering. May we all smile at the deep mystery of being, and take joy in the next breath.

More . . .

Endangered animals are those species that are in danger of becoming extinct. Since their reproductive rates are lower than their mortality rates over long periods of time, their numbers are diminishing. The reasons are varied but often involve a loss of habitat as people encroach on their living areas. Tragically, many species could be lost forever. Paleontologists estimate that well over 90 percent of all plant and animal species that ever existed have already become extinct.

Journal Prompts

—What is going on right now in world events—that include humanity, animals, and the environment—that bring you sorrow?

—Make a list of all the things you love most in nature, like the wind, orange blossoms, butterflies, etc.

—Today . . .

Day 35: Make No Sense

Logic is often a burden. Doing silly things helps shatter our self-importance and triggers relaxation.

Activity

Create an absurd activity. For example, take the kitchen dishes for a ride in your car. Give your coffee mug a name. Dig a hole in your garden for no good reason. Take everything out of your desk drawer and then put it back. Walk around the block backwards.

> *More . . .*
>
> *All phenomena change. What happens to a puddle after it rains? Where does the water go? Water on Earth is used over and over again as it evaporates and then returns as rain.*

Journal Prompts

—What risks are you willing to take to move out of your comfort zone?

—What has to change in your life for you to finally be happy?

—Today . . .

Quick Check-In:

How are you doing? What is happening to your commitment to your intention? Are you worried about it? Is your intention changing? Are you? How?

_____

_____

_____

_____

_____

_____

_____

_____

_____

_____

_____

_____

_____

_____

_____

Day 36: Look to Nature

Nature illustrates impermanence in infinite ways. What happens to a shooting star, bubbles in a stream, morning dew, or lightning? Now you see them, now you don't.

Activity

Lick your index finger and gently stroke it across your forehead, between your eyebrows. Close your eyes, wait a moment, then notice how the moisture feels as it is absorbed into the air. Water is literally evaporating into air. Melt into this sensation and experience something elemental, something that is completely out of your control.

> ## More . . .
>
> *Immediately after birth a tiny blind kangaroo joey is able to crawl up its mother's body to find the pouch intended for it. A giraffe colt enters this world while its mother is walking around. That means it falls about six feet to the ground and gets up on its feet and walks. A human infant needs about one year to find the ability to stand up on its own two feet!*

Journal Prompts

—What simple natural wonders—from ice melting to flowers blooming amaze you?

—List the most dramatic natural wonders you have experienced—from blazing sunsets to blasting hurricanes.

—Today . . .

DAY 37: CALL SOMEONE

When we don't finish emotional business it holds us back from what we need to do, and sometimes even from what we truly want. Clear the decks and begin fresh.

Activity

Call someone today, or write them a letter. Reconnect, thank, apologize, or make a clean good-bye. Create room for new things to enter.

> *More . . .*
>
> *In the olden days, the person who sent out a letter expected the recipient to pay for the cost of mailing. Since the cost of postage was relatively high, it was thought the one who benefited most from the transaction was the one who received the missive!*

Journal Prompts

—List all the people you want to call or write. What is holding you back?

—List some of your saddest good-byes.

—Today . . .

DAY 38: EVERYDAY PRAYER

Prayer is an exercise of introspection and transformation. It creates a place where a new you has the chance to emerge.

Activity

Recite prayers you've memorized or create your own and repeat throughout the entire day. Make sure you say one out loud every time you cross a threshold as you walk through doorways in your home and out into the world.

> ### More . . .
>
> *The Hebrew words for prayer, Li-heet-pallel, mean to inspect oneself. Prayer is not waving a magic wand, hoping for the best. It is not begging God to make it right for you. When we pray we look inside and question: "What do I need to change about myself in order to get what I really want out of life?"*

Journal Prompts

—Write out one prayer that you know by heart. What do you want to pray for right now?

—What bitterness or resentment still linger in your soul? Why?

—Today . . .

DAY 39: SPACE OUT

Daydreaming, zoning out, and experiencing reverie are all states of being that have value. They quiet the mind and feed the soul.

Activity

When you were young, you probably did a lot of things all by yourself. Get small and sit down on the floor, preferably under a table or even tucked in a coat closet. Or simply curl up by a window and daydream. Stare, follow an airplane trail, or watch the clouds roll by. Can you bypass the guilt of doing nothing for a few moments?

> ### More . . .
>
> *Standing is not stillness. It is perpetual movement. Tall trees are always swaying in some fashion.*

Journal Prompts

—What activities or childhood rituals brought you into deep reverie? Did you hide under the covers, sing to yourself, stare at the wallpaper?

—Were you chastised for doing nothing or being lazy?

—List the places where you really feel safe.

—Today . . .

DAY 40: STAND TALL

When humans first stood up, they created a visible link between heaven and earth. Erect we embody strength and lightness, stability and flowing balance.

Activity

Stand up tall. Place your feet solidly on the floor and imagine roots growing from your feet deep into the earth. Then imagine that a hook in the sky is attached to the very top of your head. Elongate your skull up toward the heavens and soften your knees as you lengthen your spine down to the floor. Open your arms wide, making a T-shape and reach out from your heart. Inhale and fill up your lungs. Breathe three times with arms open and eyes alert. Now allow your arms to float down to your sides. Gently feel yourself vital, centered, standing tall, and ready to take that next step!

More . . .

Your feet are made up of 26 bones that carry your entire body weight. When you stand, spread your toes wide and use the maximum amount of surface on your soles, including your toes. The bigger your base, the more solid your foundation. When you walk, notice how you need to balance on one foot before you move forward. Life is like this. It is about continually finding and refinding your balance.

Journal Prompts

—List the feelings that arise as you stand tall and gather your newfound power . . .

—Write words of congratulations to yourself and acknowledge the completion of your 40 day and 40 night excursion.

—Today . . .

AFTERWORD: BEYOND DAY 40

Re-Entry

Well, you've made it! With intention and a willingness to follow through, you have opened up, been lost, been found, and been more in touch with your intuition. Now what? It's time to reflect on what you've learned and allow it to feed the rest of your life.

Take a Moment and Reflect

Before you go any further it's a good idea to do a final check-in. Use these last pages and respond to the following journal prompts.

—Write down your original intention.

—How close did you come to making your intention a reality? Did you achieve the results you wanted?

—Why? Why not?

Now take some time and review your entries from Day one all the way through Day 40. Then respond to the following journal prompts:

—How has this piece of time inspired or informed your intention?

—What stands out as the most surprising insight, revelation, lesson, or experience?

—If a friend were to ask you to describe or summarize all that you've discovered about yourself and how you live your life, what would you say? Be verbose!

> *Remember:*
>
> *No matter what has or has not happened, your awareness is growing and your freedom of choice is expanding.*

Stay Awake and Alive

To keep what you've discovered alive past Day 40, reflect on three activities that you really enjoyed and make a commitment to incorporate them into your daily life. And to keep yourself relaxed, open, and inspired down the road, make sure you practice the following eight powerful activities guaranteed to keep you tuned in.

SOFT BELLY	pg. 47
COUNT DOWN AND SLOW DOWN	pg. 53
LISTEN TO YOUR HEART	pg. 59
FLOATING EYES	pg. 70
A E I O U	pg. 95
SHAKE IT UP	pg. 207
EVERYDAY PRAYER	pg. 241
STAND TALL	pg. 252

Bull's-Eye

There's an old story about a hunter who is walking through the woods. He comes across hundreds of large colorful targets painted on all kinds of trees and is amazed to see that *all* of the arrows on *all* of the targets have hit the bull's-eyes! Never a miss! The hunter wanders near and far, anxious to meet this perfect marksman. Finally he finds him and asks, "Please tell me, what is the secret behind your perfect aim? You never miss!" The archer smiles and replies, "It is really quite simple. *First* I shoot my arrows. *Then* I paint the targets."

Sounds like this marksman always had something to shoot for. He trusted himself and knew wherever he aimed, with clear intention and honest effort, he'd always hit his mark! All of us expect life to be about hitting the right mark, but we spend so much of our time trying to "get it right" that we often miss. The last 40 days, in many ways, are all about shooting arrows of belief and self-love. Fueled by the desire for self-knowledge and the courage to explore, you were willing to move ahead without a specific end product or finish line in sight. And yet, your target did materialize, probably in more ways than one. In your own uniquely personal way, you have discovered valuable information about yourself and how to live your life. It has taken great courage to shoot your arrows without a particular target in mind, wandering alone in your metaphorical desert, willing to look, listen, and respond to parts of yourself that you've probably never met before.

Hopefully, your discovery at the end of your 40 days and 40 nights is a deep appreciation of what is inside of you and a willingness to connect with what is around you. With this kind of trust and self-knowledge, you will always hit the bull's-eye. You just need to keep shooting, knowing full well that with honesty and heartfelt intention, your arrows will always hit home.